Wedding Sermons And Marriage Ceremonies

Derl G. Keefer

and

Cheryl Rohret

CSS Publishing Company, Inc., Lima, Ohio

Scripture quotations identified (NRSV) are from the *New Revised Standard Version of the Bible*, copyright 1989 by the Division of Christian Education of the National Council of the Churches of Christ in the USA. Used by permission.

Scripture quotations identified (TEV) are from the *Good News Bible*, in Today's English Version. Copyright © American Bible Society 1966, 1971, 1976. Used by permission.

Scripture quotations identified (RSV) are from the *Revised Standard Version of the Bible*, copyrighted 1946, 1952 ©, 1971, 1973, by the Division of Christian Education of the National Council of the Churches of Christ in the USA. Used by permission.

This book is available in the following formats, listed by ISBN:
0-7880-1573-7   Book
0-7880-1574-5   Disk
0-7880-1575-3   Sermon Prep

With grateful thanks to all the couples
who inspired these sermons,
and to Vic, the love of my life.
— Cheryl Rohret

To the lady who has
taught me what marriage
truly means — my wife Karen!
— Derl Keefer

Table Of Contents

Weddings Can Be Beautiful

The Christian envisions marriage as a God-given direction for life. Before a marriage takes place counseling is given by the minister to assist in molding, guiding, and supporting the couple in their new venture together.

Preparation of the ceremony becomes the final stage of the process. The following ceremonies are designed to provide models for the minister to choose from or to assist in creating new ones.

Some guidelines for deciding on ceremonies include:

1. Allow creative planning for the ritual.

2. Ask the couple for input.

3. Incorporate as many family and friends as possible throughout the ceremony.

4. Ask the couple for a favorite poem, scripture, or song to make the moments meaningful.

5. Request that the couple write part of their own vows.

6. Keep personal control of the rehearsal and wedding day events.

7. Make this a spiritual event in the lives of the couple and the congregation gathered to celebrate this happy occasion.

8. Stay relaxed even if some unforeseen circumstance happens. If you panic, so will the couple, and this could ruin a wonderful experience.

9. Review the ceremony before you enter the sanctuary. It will refresh your memory.

10. Above all, remember that God wants to bless this important wedding day with His presence. Don't fail to ask Him to attend!

The wedding ceremony can be a beautiful and spiritual experience!

— Derl G. Keefer

Weddings Are Celebrations

Weddings are a wonderful opportunity for couples to see how much God is involved in the love they share. Many couples who come to be married have had only a passing connection with the church. They aren't sure what faith in Jesus Christ has to do with their marriage. Rather than refusing to marry them because of their limited understanding or experience of faith in Christ, this can be a window of opportunity for a pastor. The couple can be commended for their desire to make a lasting commitment to each other before God and their families and friends. Then they can be invited in the time of counseling to explore their faith more intentionally, individually and as a couple.

These wedding sermons are a celebration of the love which brings couples together in the bond of marriage. They are also a celebration and a witness to the love of God in Christ which upholds us all.

Cheryl Rohret

Ceremony 1

Pastor: In the beginning days of creation, God was pleased with all He had created. Looking at Adam's solitude, however, God realized that humankind needs companionship, so woman came into existence. In the innocence of Eden, the marriage relationship began! God initiated this relationship because of our need for support, care, and love. Over the centuries, countless couples have searched for acceptance, love, and companionship in the womb of marriage.

Today we gather to celebrate these characteristics in the marriage of _(Groom)_ and _(Bride)_. This marriage event is in one sense a very private time for _(Groom)_ and _(Bride)_, yet it publicly speaks to everyone that _(Groom)_ and _(Bride)_ belong uniquely to each other, with no one intruding upon their relationship.

To this end we may declare with the psalmist, "I will give thanks to the Lord with my whole heart; I will tell of all thy wonderful deeds."

Pastor: *(To the Father)* Who gives this woman to be married to this man?

Father: Her family lovingly gives her to this man for a lifetime of commitment.

Pastor: If you desire your life to be touched with eternal beauty, then catch and cherish the days of your courtship. Even when showered by the commonplace experiences ahead, refuse steadfastly to allow your vision to be blurred.

God's Word declares that love, joy, hope, and goodness should be practiced by all. No place is it better to be practiced than in the home. Becoming a husband or a wife does not destroy your

9

individuality, but rather it enhances and enriches your natural skills, abilities, and talents. God will help you grow and develop as people planned in His image. As you contribute your best to one another, you will become one in life's most intimate and fulfilling relationship.

This is our prayer as we witness the beginning of your life's journey together.

Friend: Let us pray ... *(Extemporaneous or written prayer by a friend of either groom or bride)*

Pastor: What do you give as a token of your love and commitment to one another?

Couple: A ring. *(Best Man and Matron/Maid of Honor give rings to Pastor, who then hands rings to couple.)*

Pastor: *(To Groom)* Place the ring on _(Bride's)_ finger and repeat after me.

Pastor (Groom Repeats): I, _(Groom)_ , give you this ring, _(Bride)_ , out of sincere commitment. I know this ring is only a symbol, but it is a *lasting* symbol of my love.

Bride: I, _(Bride)_ , receive this ring, _(Groom)_ , as your symbol of lasting love.

Pastor: *(To Bride)* Place this ring on _(Groom's)_ finger and repeat after me.

Pastor (Bride Repeats): I, _(Bride)_ , give you this ring, _(Groom)_ , out of sincere commitment. I know this ring is only a symbol, but it is a *lasting* symbol of my love.

Groom: I, _(Groom)_ , receive this ring, _(Bride)_ , as a symbol of lasting love.

Special Music: "With This Ring" (Words and Music by Clyde Otis and Vincent Corso, Hudson Bay Music, Inc.)

Pastor: Benjamin Franklin has been credited with the thought, "It is the man and woman united that make the complete human being. Together, they are most likely to succeed in the world."

It is with this thought of unity that you come now to take your vows.

Pastor: _(Groom)_ , repeat after me:

Pastor (Groom Repeats): I, _(Groom)_ , take you, _(Bride)_ , to be my wife now and throughout the rest of our lives. I pledge my undying faithfulness and will continue to love you always.

Pastor: _(Bride)_ , repeat after me:

Pastor (Bride Repeats): I, _(Bride)_ , take you, _(Groom)_ , to be my husband now and throughout the rest of our lives. I pledge my undying faithfulness and will continue to love you always.

Special Music: "Love Will Be Our Home" (*Contemporary Christian Wedding Songbook*, Hal Leonard Corporation, Milwaukee, Wisconsin, 1995)

Pastor: _(Groom)_ and _(Bride)_ , it is now my joy, granted me by the State of _(State)_ and the _(Church)_ , to declare to all that you are husband and wife, since you have of your free will given commitments to one another. I charge you to become one in your relationship.

(Groom) , you may now kiss your bride!

Pastor: Friends, it is my pleasure to introduce to you, _(First Name)_ and _(First Name)_ _(Last Name)_ .

11

Ceremony 2

The Prologue

Pastor: Dear Friends, the greatest spiritual purpose of marriage is love. True love changes not only the world, but individual lives. We participate in marriage through the avenue of this love. We have come to witness the marriage of _(Groom)_ and _(Bride)_ who have experienced this love power.

Pastor: Who gives this woman in marriage?

Father: Her family because of our respect and consideration for _(Bride)_ and _(Groom's)_ decision to marry.

Special Music: "Parent's Prayer" (Praise Hymn Soundtracks, Nashville, Tennessee)

Pastor: _(Groom)_ and _(Bride)_, you come to this marriage ceremony today, not accidentally, but directed by Almighty God to fulfill the highest calling for each of you — a loving union.

You are here to invite God to be an active participant in your wedding. To marry is to say, "I do," and for God to say, "Yes, you do," for a lifetime.

You are about to assume mutual responsibility and relationships. Today you will pledge your undying devotion and commitment to each other. If for any reason you should *not* make this solemn covenant to each other, speak now or forever hold your peace.

Coming into this sanctuary you realize that this covenant is not just a legal contract, but a contract made in heaven. It is to be entered into with reverence and awe. You must seek God's direction. Therefore, we need to seek God in prayer.

Pastor: *(Prays extemporaneously)* ...

The Exchange Of Vows

Pastor: _(Bride)_ and _(Groom)_, join hands, and in these vows you are about to take know that there is no more lovely, friendly, and charming communion as in a good marriage partner.

Pastor: _(Groom)_, please repeat after me.

Pastor (Groom Repeats): I, _(Groom)_, take you, _(Bride)_, for my wife. I marry you today because I love you. I marry you today because you bring me joy. I marry you today because of what I know about you. I marry you today because I want to spend the rest of my life discovering more about you. I will endeavor to make your life fulfilled. I will always be here for you.

Pastor: _(Bride)_, please repeat after me.

Pastor (Bride Repeats): I, _(Bride)_, take you, _(Groom)_, for my husband. I marry you today because I love you. I marry you today because you bring me joy. I marry you today because I want to spend the rest of my life discovering more about you. I will endeavor to make your life fulfilled. I will always be here for you.

Special Music: "I Will Be Here" (Christian World, Oklahoma City, Oklahoma, 1990)

Pastoral Prayer: Our Father, _(Groom)_ has discovered the delicate balance in life loving you and loving another human being. As _(Bride)_ and _(Groom)_ unite their lives, help them to touch the heart chords of each other and yours also. As they marry, may each bring care, tenderness, kindness, and love as elixirs of life. May they bring different perspectives that will cause this marriage to be strong. May you ordain this union with your divine and holy presence from the start. May you never leave them nor forsake them — nor they you. In the name of the Holy Father, blessed Son, and Spirit of life.

The Exchange Of Rings

Pastor: Do you give rings as a symbol of your love?

Couple: Yes, we do.

Pastor: Let the never-ending circle of the ring be a reminder of your never-ending devotion and love for one another.

Couple: We promise to separate ourselves from other relationships and to keep ourselves pure for each other only.

Pastor: Let the beauty of the ring be a reminder that beauty only comes through a fire of life.

Couple: We promise to live together even when trials, failures, and adversity occur, because deep within is the fire burning hotly for life together.

The Pronouncement

Pastor: _(Groom)_ and _(Bride)_, you have found love in each other. Let nothing or no one destroy that love. Teach each other new things in this marriage of two hearts. You see the love in one another that comes straight from the heart of God. Nurture that love. Never allow it to fade, but only to shine on for the rest of your lives.

Now that you have pledged your devotion and faithfulness before God and this company, I pronounce you husband and wife by the authority of the State of _(State)_ and the _(Church)_ and the investment of God.

(Groom), you may now kiss your bride.

Pastor: Dear family and friends, it is my distinct honor to present to you _(First Name)_ and _(First Name)_ _(Last Name)_.

Ceremony 3

The Prologue

Pastor: God said, "It is not good that man should be alone; I will make a helpmeet for him" (Genesis 2:18 KJV). So from the beginning of human history man and woman have shared life together as helpers and companions. _(Groom)_ and _(Bride)_ are together because God wants them together. They have prayed and sought His will in this important matter of the heart. There is an old saying that, "A man times a wife is equal to four." They are together because the life of each is completed in the other. So it is with _(Bride)_ and _(Groom)_ , who were alone, but are no longer.

The two of you have fulfillment in life, especially with children and grandchildren, but you still have a life ahead, filled with the gift of time, cushioned by joy, hope, and love. The fervor of youth wanes; the delight of age remains. As John Killinger wrote, "There is always something young about love, young and innocent and beautiful. It has made our friends young, innocent, and beautiful together."

We gather to celebrate what God has instilled in the hearts of _(Groom)_ and _(Bride)_ and to witness their coming together as husband and wife. Make this home a haven of rest, dedicated to bringing love to anyone who enters its doors!

If any object to any of this, let them speak now or remain silent forever.

The Exchange Of Vows

Pastor: _(Groom)_ and _(Bride)_ , please join hands, look into each other's eyes, and couple your hearts as you repeat your vows.

Pastor: _(Groom)_ , please repeat after me:

Pastor (Groom Repeats): I, _(Groom)_ , take you, _(Bride)_ , for my lawfully wedded wife. I promise to love you and care for you the rest of my life. As long as God supplies strength to me, I shall endeavor to make you happy and to share the blessings from God. I marry you because I enjoy you for who you are.

Pastor: Now, (Bride) , please repeat the same vow after me:

Pastor (Bride Repeats): I, (Bride) , take you, (Groom) , for my lawfully wedded husband. I promise to love you and care for you the rest of my life. As long as God supplies strength to me, I shall endeavor to make you happy and to share the blessings from God. I marry you because I enjoy you for *who* you are.

Pastoral Prayer: Our Father, (Groom) has discovered that the highest call of man is to dedicate his life to serving God and doing good. Uniting his life with (Bride's) helps to further that purpose because of her intense dedication to the life of Christ as well.

As they marry, may each be a part of the other's life. In all decisions the other will be a part of the consideration of the solution. In all problems the other will be a factor to understand. In all joy they will share and in all sorrow be a support to one another. Together they start life with love — a love that you bless and ordain. Let your blessing rest upon them forever. In the name of the Father, Son, and Holy Spirit. Amen.

The Exchange Of Rings
Pastor: (Groom) , please place on (Bride's) finger the ring you give her as a symbol of your devotion to her, and continuing to look into her eyes, repeat after me:

Pastor (Groom Repeats): (Bride) , I give you this ring as a symbol of my love. May it remain always to you and to others a symbol of my fidelity, and may God graciously bless our marriage.

Pastor: (Bride) , please repeat after me your words of acceptance.

Pastor (Bride Repeats): (Groom) , I accept your ring and will wear it as a symbol of my fidelity, and I know God will graciously bless our marriage.

Pastor: _(Bride)_ , please place on _(Groom's)_ finger the ring you give him as a symbol of your devotion to him, and continuing to look into his eyes, repeat after me:

Pastor: (Bride Repeats): _(Groom)_ , I give you this ring as a symbol of my love. May it remain always to you and to others a symbol of my fidelity, and may God graciously bless our marriage.

Pastor: _(Groom)_ , please repeat after me your words of acceptance.

Pastor (Groom Repeats): _(Bride)_ , I accept your ring and will wear it as a symbol of my fidelity, and I know God will graciously bless our marriage.

The Pronouncement

Pastor: _(Groom)_ and _(Bride)_ , you have found each other in the mature years of your life on earth. You will teach each other new things in this union of two people and two spirits. You see the miracle in one another that is invisible to others. _You_ are a miracle to one another. Nurture the miracle of married love. May it never fade, but only brighten in the years ahead.

Now that you have pledged your love and faithfulness to each other, I take great pleasure in pronouncing you husband and wife by the authority of the _(Church)_ , and the investment of God, and the State of _(State)_ . Will you grace this pronouncement with a kiss?

The Blessing

Pastor: Let us pray as you begin this journey:

O God, who does not desire for man or woman to be alone in heart and spirit, but joins them together that they should live and love and worship You, we join You in this celebration of marriage of our friends _(Groom)_ and _(Bride)_ . Let each of their days on earth be long and filled to overflowing with love and excitement for one another. Give them the joy of simple moments spent together in music, over the kitchen table, walking in a shopping mall, looking at old photographs, holding hands, giving thanks for each other, and attending your house of worship. Bless their children and grandchildren that they may find happiness in the new relationships that have come to them, and in their parents' happiness. Oh, God, our hearts rejoice in love! Amen.

Special Music: "The Lord's Prayer"

Pastor: It is my pleasure to introduce to you __(First Name)__ and __(First Name)__ __(Last Name)__.

Ceremony 4

The Prologue

Pastor: Dear Friends, today __(Groom)__ and __(Bride)__ have come to this moment with love in their heart. __(Bride)__ and __(Groom)__, you have been drawn together with an attraction that should continue throughout your life time. No longer will you be looking with separate visions for life but rather with one vision. You will retain your individuality, but you will discover unity of purpose for each other. You are performing an act of faith in each other, and in God who has brought your love together. __(Groom)__, you are to be to __(Bride)__ protector, caregiver, mate, and, most sacred, husband. __(Bride)__, you are to be to __(Groom)__ an inspiration, sustainer, mate, and, most sacred, wife.

If your life is to be successful, it will be done as God is asked to control and guide it. Allow God to mold your lives together to form a beautiful duet of love. Human imperfections will appear where dating bliss first blurred your sight. Remain unmoved in your love for each other. Imperfection and faults can be overcome with time, patience, and devotion to one another. Let God be the perceptible presence in your home. Also, allow your home to be a harbor of rest and repair from the pressures of the world.

Special Music: "How Beautiful" (The Benson Co., Nashville, Tennessee, 1990)

Pastor: *(Prays extemporaneously)* ...

Pastor: *(To Father)* Who gives this woman to be married to this man?

Father: Her family who loves her. We welcome __(Groom)__ into our family and we pledge to love them both. Our family covenants to support them with our love and prayers, and help when appropriate. *(Father gives bride a kiss and then joins the hands of bride and groom.)*

The Exchange Of Vows And Rings

Pastor: Now, (Groom) and (Bride) , we are coming to the solemn moment when you exchange vows and make a covenant of love to each other.

These vows are important because they are set in the context of God and his people. Covenants are binding and not to be entered into lightly or irreverently. There will be times of doubt and insecurity, but stand steady — your love for each other and God will hold your love tightly together.

Are you willing to continue the taking of these sacred vows?

Couple: Yes, we are. Let the vows be binding upon us for the rest of our lives.

Pastor: (Groom) , please place the ring upon (Bride's) finger and repeat these vows after me.

Pastor (Groom Repeats): I, (Groom) , take you, (Bride) , as my dearly beloved wife. I covenant before God, to care for you as long as we both shall live. I will place your well-being at the head of my personal agenda. I pledge my love for you in front of these people, this minister, and God. I shall pray that our lives will become one together. I will do my best to pursue God's will and purpose for our journey together.

Pastor: (Bride) , please place the ring upon (Groom's) finger, and repeat these vows.

Pastor (Bride Repeats): I, (Bride) , take you, (Groom) , as my beloved husband. I covenant before God, to care for you as long as we both shall live. I will place your well-being at the head of my personal agenda. I pledge my love for you in front of these people, this minister, and God. I, too, shall pray that our lives will truly become one together. I will do my best to pursue God's will and purpose for our journey together.

Pastor: _(Groom)_ and _(Bride)_, your families, friends, and God have witnessed these moments of commitment and given their blessings to this union. You together have pledged your undying love to one another. Therefore, upon the authority of the church and the state I declare you husband and wife.

(Groom) and _(Bride)_, you may seal your marriage with a kiss.

I have the great privilege to introduce for the first time _(First Name)_ and _(First Name)_ _(Last Name)_.

What God has joined together let nothing destroy!

Benediction

Pastor: May the God who has given you the miracle of marriage, guard your future and fill the days with joy, happiness, and hope with each other and the God of holy marriages. Go in peace and love!

Ceremony 5

Pastor: Welcome to the wedding of __(Groom)__ and __(Bride)__ . They have discovered that the many-faceted dimensions of love include the spiritual dimension. Love's power can transform the world. Many times we find the level of love that is so emotional and social, but there is a loftier dimension. God is in the midst of this kind of love. He is the weaver with the thread of gold. Through marriage we invite the highest spiritual experience in the eternal joy of love.

__(Bride)__ and __(Groom)__ desire to embody the highest values of life in their relationship as God is brought into this marriage today, creating a loving union.

Who brings this woman to this moment of love?

Father: Her family brings her to this love friendship that is set on fire for a lifetime.

Pastor: A husband and wife should bear each other's joys, sorrows, burdens, and hope. As you enter marriage, you are cultivating a new life together. The elements of consideration, love, and tender-heartedness should be planted for a lifetime.

As Randolph Ray wrote, "I would like to have engraved inside every wedding band, 'Be kind to one another.' This is the Golden Rule of marriage and the secret of making love last through the years."

So, __(Groom)__ and __(Bride)__ , I charge you to love one another with a deep, abiding love. The vows you are about to take are to bond you for a lifetime.

Pastor: __(Groom)__ , repeat after me.

Pastor (Groom Repeats): I marry you, __(Bride)__ , because I want you to be a part of my life. I pledge that you will be a part of my

22

decisions and considerations in life. I will share my joy and ask for your support in sorrow for as long as we both shall live. _(Bride)_ , I love you!

Pastor: _(Bride)_ , repeat after me:

Pastor (Bride Repeats): I accept your pledge of love. I marry you, _(Groom)_ , because I want you to be a part of my life. I pledge to you that you will be part of my decisions and considerations in my life. I will share my joy and ask for your support in sorrow for as long as we both shall live. _(Groom)_ , I love you!

Groom: I accept your pledge of love.

Pastor: God is the center of life. He has no beginning and no ending, just like these rings. Let the seamlessness of the circle be a symbol of your endless love.

Groom: _(Bride)_ , I give you this ring as my symbol of never-ending steadfastness as I respect you for the rest of my life.

Bride: _(Groom)_ , I give you this ring as my symbol of never-ending steadfastness as I respect you for the rest of my life.

Special Music: "Perfect Union" (by John Andrew Schreiner and Matthew Ward, _Contemporary Christian Wedding Songbook_, a Hal Leonard Corporation, 1995)

Pastor: As a Christian couple, _(Bride)_ and _(Groom)_ would like to begin their marriage with communion to signify their love for God. This time will help set a pattern for their new journey and give them a sense of commitment to their holy God. We open to all who are members of God's family of faith, the meal of redemption.

(Ushers will come and pass to the wedding party and members of the congregation the communion elements.)

Pastor: Let us recall on that night so long ago how the Lord Jesus, on the night of betrayal, took bread and blessed it and distributed it to all of his disciples and said, "Take, eat; this is my body broken for you. This do in remembrance of me." He then took a cup and blessed it and said, "This cup is the new covenant in my blood. Take, drink it, if you are able." As often as we eat this bread and drink this cup, we commemorate the Lord's death until he returns."

Pastoral Prayer Of Thanksgiving

Pastor: (Groom) and (Bride) , your love for each other has drawn you together. In this sanctuary and in the sanctuaries of your hearts, you have become one in love. Therefore, by the authority of the (Church) and the State of (State) , I pronounce that you are husband and wife. May your lives forever be entwined and may God sanctify your marriage. (Groom) , you may now kiss your bride.

Pastor: It is my distinct honor to introduce to this congregation (First Name) and (First Name)   (Last Name) . What God has joined together let no person separate.

Ceremony 6

Pastor: The world we live in changes constantly; governments rise and fall; institutions expand and falter. Marriage remains one of the stabilizing foundations in the world. It delivers joy and excitement in a desperately lonely world. When Adam was alone in the ancient garden, God knew that man needed someone with whom to develop a relationship, so Eve became the companion for Adam. God took the initiative in the formation of marriage because of the need for a deep supportive relationship between a man and a woman. Since that first union of love, millions of people have sought love, acceptance, and companionship in the relationship we call marriage.

Today, we are witnesses to a very private moment in the lives of _(Groom)_ and _(Bride)_, as we celebrate publicly this union with thanksgiving.

Who gives this woman to be married to this man?

Father: Her mother and I, who gave her life and grace. We stamped our image upon her life by carving ideas, thoughts, philosophy, and spirit into her heart. When she was a child we calmed her fears, bandaged her knees, and kissed her hurts. She sat on our laps and we read her favorite books. Today we share her with the man she loves, _(Groom)_, because we love her so.

Pastor: _(Bride)_ and _(Groom)_, if you desire for your new relationship to be a thing of beauty, allow God to make your home a place of repair and a harbor of security. Always believe in the ideal in each other. Follow God's divine principle of love.

Friend Of The Couple Will Read 1 Corinthians 13 from *The Living Bible*

Special Music: "This is the Day" (by Scott Wesley Brown, *Contemporary Christian Wedding Songbook*, Hal Leonard Corporation, Milwaukee, Wisconsin, 1995)

Pastor: As the bride gives herself to the bridegroom, let him be to her a most sacred husband. As the groom gives himself to the bride, let her be to him a most sacred wife.

Will you exchange vows with each other?

Couple: We will.

Groom: _(Bride)_ , I pledge to you my undying love and faith. I promise to respect you. I dedicate my time, talent, and treasures to you. I give myself fully as husband to discover joy and pleasure with you. God took special care crafting you for me, and I will treasure you for the rest of my life.

Bride: _(Groom)_ , I pledge to you my undying love and faith. I promise to respect you. I dedicate my time, talent, and treasures to you. I give myself fully as wife to discover joy and pleasure with you. God took special care in crafting you for me, and I will treasure you for the rest of my life.

Pastor: Let us pray ... *(Prays extemporaneously, followed by "The Lord's Prayer" in song)*

Pastor: Do you have rings for a pledge or promise?

Couple: We do.

Pastor: _(Groom)_ , look into _(Bride's)_ eyes and place your ring of promise on her finger as you repeat after me.

Pastor (Groom Repeats): I, _(Groom)_ , take you, _(Bride)_ , to be my life's companion. This ring is my promise that you will always be in my heart, and I will cherish and honor you all the days of my life.

Bride: I accept this ring from you, _(Groom)_ , as a pledge of promised love.

26

Pastor: _(Bride)_ , look into _(Groom's)_ eyes and place your ring of promise on his finger as you repeat after me.

Pastor (Bride Repeats): I, _(Bride)_ , take you, _(Groom)_ , to be my life's companion. This ring is my promise that you will always be in my heart, and I will cherish and honor you all the days of my life.

Groom: I accept this ring from you, _(Bride)_ , as a pledge of promised love.

Pastor: _(Groom)_ and _(Bride)_ , you may each take a candle to symbolize your individual lives. Use these candles to light the center candle as a symbol of your new lives of unity starting today. A family does not eliminate separate individuality, but enhances and enriches this most intimate relationship.

Special Music: "Love Will Be Our Home" (by Stephen Curtis Chapman, _Contemporary Christian Wedding Songbook_, Hal Leonard Corporation, Milwaukee, Wisconsin, 1995)

Pastor: _(Bride)_ and _(Groom)_ , your love has brought you to this sanctuary, and God has blessed this day. Since you have exchanged vows and rings, I pronounce you husband and wife by the authority of _(Church)_ and the state of _(State)_ . What God has joined together let no one put asunder. _(Groom)_ , you may now kiss your bride.

Ladies and gentlemen it is my pleasure to introduce to you for the very first time, _(First Name)_ and _(First Name)_ _(Last Name)_ .

Ceremony 7

Pastor: Mr. and Mrs. _(Groom's parents' name)_ , Mr. and Mrs. _(Bride's parents' name)_ , friends, and witnesses, we have gathered here to celebrate the marriage of _(Groom)_ and _(Bride)_ , who have fallen in love and willingly chosen this occasion to pledge publicly their vows to each other.

They have discovered their individual love has purpose and fulfillment in each other. Their desire is to cultivate the conditions of that love and to fulfill its highest meaning. _(Bride)_ and _(Groom)_ know that God has impregnated that love with his divine destiny for them. In this spirit they are not marrying because of their physical attraction for one another, but because they want to experience God's best for their lives together.

We come to celebrate with them this glowing love. Each of us here is incredibly happy and filled with joy for this occasion of marriage of _(Groom)_ and _(Bride)_ .

Pastoral Prayer: All-mighty, knowing God, we come in your presence today asking for a special blessing upon _(Bride)_ and _(Groom)_ . Join them in their destiny throughout the rest of their lives. As they give verbal vows and hear from each other's heart, may they know that their lives will center in each other and in you. May their hearts sing for joy and happiness now and forever! Amen.

Solo: "Grow Old With Me" (by John Lennon)

Pastor: _(Groom)_ , do you take _(Bride)_ to be your wife as you begin your marital journey? Do you promise to give your whole self to her completely? Do you promise to tell her how much you love her — often? Do you covenant to gaze into her heart but look outward at life together in the same direction? Will you forsake every other relationship and be devoted to her? If so say, "I do."

Groom: I do.

Pastor: _(Bride)_ , do you take _(Groom)_ to be your husband as you begin your marital journey? Do you promise to give your whole self to him completely? Do you promise to tell him how much you love him — often? Do you covenant to gaze into his heart but look outward at life together in the same direction? Will you forsake every other relationship and be devoted to him? If so say, "I do."

Bride: I do.

Children Of The Couple Will Read From 1 Corinthians 13

Reader 1: Love is patient and kind, Love is not jealous

Reader 2: Or conceited, or proud, or provoked;

Reader 3: Love does not keep a record of wrongs;

Reader 1: Love is not happy with evil

Reader 2: But is pleased with the truth.

Reader 3: Love never gives up;

Readers: _(Unison)_ Its faith, hope, patience never fails.

Pastor: Do you have rings?

Couple: Yes, we do.

(Pastor takes the rings from the Best Man and Maid of Honor)

Pastor: The circle of this ring symbolizes the never-ending trust, hope, and love that _(Groom)_ and _(Bride)_ have for one another.

Pastor: _(Groom)_ , place this ring on _(Bride's)_ finger and repeat after me.

Pastor (Groom Repeats): I, _(Groom)_ , take you, _(Bride)_ , to be my wife as a gift from God to treasure for the rest of my life.

Pastor: _(Bride)_ , place this ring on _(Groom's)_ finger and repeat after me.

Pastor (Bride Repeats): I, _(Bride)_ , take you, _(Groom)_ , to be my husband as a gift from God to treasure for the rest of my life.

Solo: "With This Ring" (by Clyde Otis and Vincent Corso, Hudson Bay Music, Inc.)

Prayer Of Thanksgiving By Family Friend

Lighting Of The Unity Candle By Couple   ·
(as a reading from **Sonnets from the Portugese** by Elizabeth Barrett Browning is read):

> _How do I love thee? Let me count the ways._
> _I love thee to the depth and breadth and height my soul can reach, when feeling out of sight for the end of being and ideal grace. I love thee to the level of every day's most quiet need, by sun and candlelight. I love thee freely, as they turn from praise. I love thee with passion put to use in my old griefs, and with my child-hood faith. I love thee with a love I seemed to lose with my lost saints. I love thee with the breath, smiles, tears, of all my life! And, if God chooses, I shall but love thee after death._

Instrumental Music: "You Light Up My Life"

Pastor: _(To Congregation)_ Will you lend your hearts and concerns to this couple and their children, upholding them in prayer and encouraging them in their new life?

Congregation: Yes, we will.

Pastor: Since you have exchanged vows and rings with each other before this congregation of witnesses, I declare by the authority of the (Church) and the state of (State) that you are husband and wife. What God has joined together let no one separate. (Groom) , you may now kiss your bride.

It is my distinct honor to present to you (First Name) and (First Name)   (Last Name) .

Recessional: "Wedding March" (by Mendelsohn)

Lighting The Unity Candle

Paul, the Apostle, once wrote a letter to his Christian friends in Corinth about the nature of true love. Hear his words as they are found in 1 Corinthians 13 (TEV):

> *Love is patient and kind; it is not jealous or conceited or proud; love is not ill-mannered or selfish or irritable; love does not keep a record of wrongs; love is not happy with evil, but is happy with the truth. Love never gives up; and its faith, hope, and patience never fail.*
> *Love is eternal.*

Eternal love. That is what you will be pledging to each other in front of all your family and friends today, __(Bride)__ and __(Groom)__. "As long as we both shall live," you will say. We are talking about something really strong here: a love that will last your whole lives long. The strange thing is, as strong as your love for one another is, remember there is something fragile about this strong love you have. It will need a lot of care.

Think about the symbolism of the unity candle you will be lighting. Eternal love between a couple begins with two individuals standing strong on their own, like the two candles burning brightly on the communion table right now. The large candle in the middle represents a new life about to be formed. (No, I'm not talking about children, yet.) I'm talking about your new life together as a couple committed to one another in marriage. The big candle stands for your marriage relationship. It will receive its light not from random sparks of romance, though that may have been what brought you together in the first place. This middle candle will come to light by your own careful choosing. Two strong individuals, you two, are choosing today to share your energy and love to create a marriage.

It used to be that after lighting the unity candle, couples would blow out the side candles, to symbolize the merging of their lives in this one relationship. But I think it is healthy for you to keep all the candles lit, as a reminder that you are still two strong individuals who will need to choose daily to put your energy into this new creation called "marriage." That is where the patience, kindness, unselfishness, and honesty of which Paul speaks come in. You will need all those things and more to keep your love and your marriage strong. I hope you don't see your marriage as a desperate necessity or a losing of self-identity. A good marriage is a wonderful choice that you make to keep on loving one another.

One thing you might note as you look at these candles is that none of them are burning at both ends. There will be times in your marriage when one or both of you will be extremely busy. You may feel like you just pass each other on the go. Short stints of that can actually be invigorating. But if that becomes the pattern of your married life, watch out. A candle burning at both ends doesn't last long. When all your energy is going toward your own individual stuff, who is going to trim the wick and keep the flame going in your marriage? That's not the job of the wife alone, or the husband alone. Marriage is a two-person job. And it takes time. Give yourselves time, __(Bride)__ and __(Groom)__. Don't burn your candles at both ends.

There is one flaw in using candles as a symbol of your eternal love. Candles have a very limited life span. But then, in the whole scope of things, so do we. How can we get eternal love from mortal beings like ourselves? That is when we need to look beyond the candles to the cross. Christ was God's eternal love come to dwell with us, showing us the way to live with a love that does last forever. __(Bride)__ and __(Groom)__, as you vow to share your love with each other forever, remember the Source of eternal love. Add the energy of God's great love for you to your love for each other and nothing can stop your marriage from burning bright and warm forever.

God be with you and give to you that love which is eternal.

34

Faith, Hope, And Love

Listen to these words of encouragement from Paul's First Letter to the Corinthians, chapter 13 (TEV):

> *Love is patient and kind; it is not jealous or conceited or proud; love is not ill-mannered or selfish or irritable; love does not keep a record of wrongs; love is not happy with evil, but is happy with the truth. Love never gives up; and its faith, hope, and patience never fail.*
>
> *Love is eternal ... What I know now is only partial; then it will be complete — as complete as God's knowledge of me.*
>
> *Meanwhile these three remain: faith, hope, and love; and the greatest of these is love.*

Sometimes when I read this passage, I think, "Nothing like stating the obvious, Paul. Of course, love is the most important thing." Love is what brings you here today, __(Bride)__ and __(Groom)__. We all know that. The two heart-shaped candelabra speak of the love that shines out from you for one another.

We know that faith is part of why you are here, too. To have faith in something or someone is to trust. It is obvious that you both do trust each other. Your faith in one another has grown stronger as you have already stood by each other through some rough times.

We know that you have hope, too. As you make your promises today, behind all the words are all your hopes for the future: hopes about careers, hopes about where you will live, hopes about how your relationship will grow and flourish, maybe even hopes for a family someday. Those hopes are so important. They will help to keep you moving into the future, instead of getting stuck in the mistakes and disappointments of the past.

So, if faith, hope, and love are so obvious, why does Paul even mention them, and why do we bring his words up here?

Two reasons. One is that it is a lot easier to *talk* about faith, hope, and love than to live by them. I think that is why Paul gets down to the nitty-gritty about love. His words help to bring it back down from candles and hearts to real life, as if to say, "Okay, _ (Bride)_ and _(Groom)_ , after all the candles are extinguished and the hearts go back to the florist, here is what real love looks like: it's being patient, humble, considerate, unselfish, and truthful." Not very glamorous, is it? Sounds like hard work, doesn't it? It is! But it is worth it!

There is another reason Paul talks about love. Not only does he want to bring it back down to earth. At the same time, he wants to point our attention back up to God. Because the kind of love Paul was talking about is more than romantic love, greater than even the warm companionship that is so special between lifelong partners. Paul is talking about a love in which you actually forget yourself and are willing to sacrifice life itself for another person, just as Jesus did in going to the cross.

In ordinary people like us, that kind of love is nothing short of a miracle. It is a gift which becomes part of us only by God's grace. To have that kind of self-giving love takes faith in more than yourselves. It requires faith in God: faith that God exists, faith that Jesus Christ is proof of God's sacrificial love, and faith that God can give you the ability to love each other at that higher level. Such love will bring a different kind of hope to your marriage, too: a hope that simply cannot be put out, no matter what happens in the years ahead. Even death can't extinguish this hope, because God's love shown in the Risen Christ points us to life beyond death.

_ (Bride)_ and _(Groom)_ , my prayer for you is that you will seek God's most excellent gift of love for your lives, and so discover those things that are truly eternal: faith, hope, and love. And the greatest of these is love.

Eternal Love

Paul, the Apostle, once wrote a letter to his Christian friends in Corinth about the nature of true love. Hear his words as they are found in 1 Corinthians 13 (TEV):

> *Love is patient and kind; it is not jealous or conceited or proud; love is not ill-mannered or selfish or irritable; love does not keep a record of wrongs; love is not happy with evil, but is happy with the truth. Love never gives up; and its faith, hope, and patience never fail.*
> *Love is eternal.*

"Love" — what a world of meanings there are in that one word. You said that word to each other, __(Bride)__ and __(Groom)__, and look what happened! Here you are, ready to commit yourselves to a lifetime of loving one another. We are excited for you! Here are all these friends and family to cheer you on and encourage you as you begin this new level of commitment to one another. Right now, eternity sounds almost manageable. Your love has you looking into the future with delight and expectation. And that is just how it should be, for the basis of a life-long marriage can be nothing less than a love that will last through eternity. As you begin married life, here are a couple of reminders about eternal love.

One thing you have already discovered is that eternal love is not easy. Paul wrote his words about love to a group of people who were discovering that it is easier to talk about love than to live it. It wasn't that they hated one another. They each just got so concerned about proving that their way was right that they forgot to give leeway for anyone else's point of view. They needed a reminder of what brought them together in the first place. Not their own opinions, good as they may have seemed. Not just nice feelings about each other. What brought them together was something outside themselves, and that was the love of God in Jesus Christ.

There will be days when the two of you will need to remind yourselves from where your love comes. Some days you may look across the breakfast table at one another in all your morning glory and think, "Eternity? Oh my!" In those moments, it will be good to remember that eternal love is more than the sum of your feelings for each other at any particular moment. Then it would be good to remember Paul's words about the kind of love that could hold together a church of arguing Corinthians, and can hold together your marriage.

That leads us to the next point: eternal love is not easy because it is not particularly natural to us. We all like to think that we are naturally patient, kind, unselfish, humble, and honest. But the truth is, there are times when we would just as soon close the book on Paul's words about love. Who can ever live up to them perfectly? Not one of us. We need to admit that, to ourselves and to one another. When you've blown it, don't go acting like you haven't. "Love is not happy with evil, but is happy with the truth." It is in the safety of your love for each other that you can come face to face with your own human frailties and still know that you are accepted. Let the God-given gift of forgiveness be offered often in your marriage and in your home.

God-given gift, I said. That, finally, is the key to eternal love. It isn't easy. It isn't natural. But it is possible, at least in part. Eternal love is a gift which God works in human hearts. This love you have for one another, (Bride) and (Groom) , is God's free gift to you. Nurture it. Share it with your children. Help it to grow. And don't forget the Giver, for all love ultimately comes from God.

May God give both of you the faith, hope, and love it takes to make your vows of eternal love a reality.

Building A Marriage
(for a couple fixing up a house)

Listen to these words from the First Letter of Paul to the Corinthians, chapter 13 (NRSV):

> *Love is patient; love is kind; love is not envious or boast-*
> *ful or arrogant or rude. It does not insist on its own*
> *way; it is not irritable or resentful; it does not rejoice*
> *in wrongdoing, but rejoices in the truth. It bears all*
> *things, believes all things, hopes all things, endures all*
> *things.*
>   *Love never ends ... When I was a child, I spoke like*
> *a child, I thought like a child, I reasoned like a child;*
> *when I became an adult, I put an end to childish ways.*
> *For now we see in a mirror, dimly, but then we will see*
> *face to face. Now I know only in part; then I will know*
> *fully, even as I have been fully known. And now faith,*
> *hope, and love abide, these three; and the greatest of*
> *these is love.*

Congratulations, _(Bride)_ and _(Groom)_ ! A few years back, would you ever have guessed that your acquaintance with each other would grow into a friendship and your friendship would grow into love? Now here you are, ready to let your love grow into a lifelong commitment. God does work in amazing ways!

Congratulations, also, on being new homeowners. In many ways, buying your first house is a lot like beginning a marriage. For one thing, it is not a matter of starting from nothing. You will be moving into a house that already has a history behind it. There are probably things that you really like about its design. There are probably other little aspects of your new home that you wouldn't have chosen to include if you had been in on the original planning and building. But you will learn to work around those things, be-cause you appreciate having a house to make into a home.

Just so, the two of you come into this new marriage relationship with different histories, different ways of being in families, different personalities. In the context of your love for one another, those differences can be interesting and exciting. They can add a lot of spark to your life together. Looked at in a positive way, you will be amazed as you continue to discover new bits and pieces about each other's background that help you put together another part of the puzzle that your partner will sometimes seem to you. Be sure to let each other know what things you love about one another as you learn to work around the little imperfections you discover. Stop often and appreciate the wonder of sharing your love and lives with one another. Not everyone has that.

Another similarity between making a home and making a marriage is that both take time. You probably have some ideas about how you want to paint, furnish, and decorate your new home. The temptation is to want to do it all now. Your impatience may lead to frustration, especially if you think your partner isn't cooperating the way you think he or she should. I've heard more couples say they have just about ended their marriages over trying to wallpaper the bathroom together.

Either the Apostle Paul had also tried decorating a house with others, or he just understood human nature very well. His love reminders are worth remembering: love is first of all patient; then kind; it doesn't rejoice when the other person makes a mistake (the old "I told you so" trap), but rejoices in the truth. Give to one another these gifts of love: time, kindness, forgiveness, and honesty.

Do you know what makes a house into a beautiful home and a marriage into a lifelong commitment? It is the love. Ultimately, it doesn't matter whether your house is furnished in early Salvation Army or in priceless antiques. Friends will want to come to your home when they sense that it is filled with love.

Love that lasts is not something any of us can create on our own. It is a gift which God gives us to nurture and develop. Take care of the gift, (Bride) and (Groom) . Remember to thank and honor the Giver. And may God give you the power and joy to keep sharing your love in a marriage built to last for all time.

Deciding To Love

(for a marriage after divorce)

Listen to these words of Scripture as they are found in Paul's
First Letter to the Corinthians, chapter 13 (NRSV):

> *Love is patient; love is kind; love is not envious or boast-*
> *ful or arrogant or rude. It does not insist on its own*
> *way; it is not irritable or resentful; it does not rejoice*
> *in wrongdoing, but rejoices in the truth. It bears all*
> *things, believes all things, hopes all things, endures all*
> *things.*
> *Love never ends ... When I was a child, I spoke like*
> *a child, I thought like a child, I reasoned like a child;*
> *when I became an adult, I put an end to childish ways.*
> *For now we see in a mirror, dimly, but then we will see*
> *face to face. Now I know only in part; then I will know*
> *fully, even as I have been fully known. And now faith,*
> *hope, and love abide, these three; and the greatest of*
> *these is love.*

Just think, (Bride) and (Groom) , about a year ago, you
each thought you could never love again. You had been hurt and
disappointed by "love." But the end of previous relationships did
not mean the end of love. Paul was right: "Love never ends." And
so we rejoice to be here with you to celebrate God's healing in
your hearts and the wonderful reawakening of love you have discovered with one another. We thank God for new beginnings.

 (Bride) and (Groom) , you already know that love is more
than feeling happy when you are together; more than holding hands
in the moonlight; more than whispering sweet words and promis-
ing to cherish each other forever. Those things are all great! I hope
you are experiencing all of them often as you are with one another,
because romance and happiness go a long way in a marriage.

But they are like the topping on a dessert: light and pleasant, but not necessarily of lasting value on their own. What you want to focus on as you prepare to say your vows to one another are those things that will give real substance to your life together. To find, as an English professor I had used to say, "the real meat and potatoes of the subject." What are the things that make for fulfilling, lasting love?

According to 1 Corinthians 13, there are some things you will have to let go — little things like rudeness, selfishness, and irritability. "Pass the salt," said with a snarl across the table after a hard day may be forgiven now and then, but if that becomes the manner in which you address your loved one day after day, love may fade and become no more than a dream.

What you will want to add more of to your marriage are simple things like patience and kindness, honesty, humility, and endurance. These are not complicated ideas. The complications arise because we often get to thinking those are the attitudes which the *other* person needs to develop. Paul is suggesting we need to be mature and look at our own attitudes first. To ask ourselves, "What do *I* need to do to be more loving?"

Love is less a feeling in God's way of defining it, than it is a decision and an action: to decide to stick with the other person even when he or she at this moment is driving you crazy; to decide that forgiveness is better than holding a grudge, even when you have been hurt; to decide for a soft answer or a kind word of encouragement, rather than the cutting comment that first comes to your tongue.

It isn't easy, this kind of love Paul speaks of so eloquently. In fact, without God's help, it is impossible. Such unselfish love is not something we can manufacture on our own. It is a gift, given only to those who are willing to make the commitment to seek God's very best.

The amazing thing is that once you have begun to receive God's love and give it to each other, you may find you just can't stop it. Others around you will begin to see the difference in you and in the way you treat them. The honesty, patience, and unselfishness you show may encourage similar responses in others. Like ripples on a pond, love spreads and touches others in indirect ways you may never even realize. "Love never ends."

 (Bride) and (Groom) , God has shown you what is possible in your love for each other. I pray that God will give you all the faith, hope, and love you need to continue experiencing God's eternal love, in your marriage and in every other part of your lives. Amen.

1 Corinthians 13; 14:1

On The Right Track
(for a long-time relationship)

The Apostle Paul writes about how real love can be recognized and nurtured. Hear these words from 1 Corinthians 13 and 14:1 (TEV):

> *Love is patient and kind; it is not jealous or conceited or proud; love is not ill-mannered or selfish or irritable; love does not keep a record of wrongs; love is not happy with evil, but is happy with the truth. Love never gives up; and its faith, hope, and patience never fail.*
>
> *Love is eternal ... When I was a child, my speech, feelings, and thinking were all those of a child; now that I am an adult, I have no more use for childish ways. What we see now is like a dim image in a mirror; then we shall see face-to-face. What I know now is only partial; then it will be complete — as complete as God's knowledge of me.*
>
> *Meanwhile these three remain: faith, hope, and love; and the greatest of these is love.*
>
> *It is love, then, that you should strive for.*

Can you believe it, (Bride) and (Groom) ? After all those years, the moment has finally come to pledge your love to one another before God and everybody. I don't know who's more excited: you two or everyone around you! You have made a long, steady journey to this moment, working toward it with a lot of patience and planning. More than many young couples getting married, you two seem to know about setting goals and working toward them. You know how to strive for what you want. The question is, what will the two of you strive for now that you are finally married?

You've done some car racing recently, and that is not a bad image for thinking about how a marriage works. No race begins

44

just when the starting gun goes off. There is a great deal of preparation behind the scenes, before the car ever drives onto the track. The driver, the crew, the car, all need to be in top condition and working together to run a good race.

A marriage never begins on the wedding day, either. It begins when two people realize they love and trust each other. So they begin to share more and more of their lives with one another, from their deepest dreams and hopes to the most mundane details of everyday life. You two have learned a great deal about each other in the years you have been together. You are becoming quite a team, and all your preparation cannot help but be in your favor as you begin your marriage.

But, of course, you can't stop now. The same effort you have given to getting to know each other before this day needs to be given in keeping your love strong from this day forward. Taking care of your love will require ongoing effort. It takes everyday maintenance. Here is where a race car and a marriage are very different. Maybe you can put your race car away for the winter and not pay much attention to it until next spring, but you can't do that with a marriage relationship. After the honeymoon is over, there will be the temptation to become completely involved in your work and in home maintenance, and all those other things that make sharing loving moments with each other seem like a luxury. If you find yourselves saying things like, "I love you so much and won't it be great when we can spend time with each other next June on our vacation. Gotta go now ...," well, it's time to get your lives off the fast track and do some preventive maintenance for your relationship.

Love is kept strong by those day-to-day gestures of kindness you give one another which say, "I think you are great and I'm glad we're together." The hug, the smile, the shared silliness, the chore done without asking, the surprise gift — sometimes it is the little things that make the difference between an okay marriage and a great marriage.

Still, there will be times when it will feel like you are both on this race track called "life" in separate cars. You are aiming for the same goal — the nice home, the family, the "good life," but you almost feel in competition with one another. (No, *I'm* more tired than you are!) It is then that you will need to take a fresh look at what it is you really want to strive for. The Apostle Paul says the most important thing to strive for is love. Not just any kind of love, but a love that is defined as self-giving rather than self-serving.

I don't believe any of us can sustain that kind of unselfish love naturally. It is a gift which God gives to us. As you begin your life as a married couple, I pray that you will let God become a third partner in your marriage. For with God involved, you will discover a love more powerful and far-reaching in the good it brings than you can even imagine. Make Christ's kind of love your aim, and your marriage will stay on the right track. God be with you, now and always.

To Join Your Paths

(for a widowed/divorced, older couple)

Hear these words from Scripture as they are found in the Book of Ruth, chapter 1, verses 16-17 (RSV):

> *But Ruth said, "Entreat me not to leave you or to return from following you; for where you go I will go, and where you lodge I will lodge; your people shall be my people, and your God my God; where you die I will die, and there will I be buried. May the Lord do so to me and more also if even death parts me from you."*

Also hear these words from 1 Corinthians 13 (RSV):

> *Love is patient and kind; love is not jealous or boastful; it is not arrogant or rude. Love does not insist on its own way; it is not irritable or resentful; it does not rejoice at wrong, but rejoices in the right. Love bears all things, believes all things, hopes all things, endures all things.*
> *Love never ends ...*
> *... So faith, hope, love abide, these three; but the greatest of these is love.*

　(Bride)　and　(Groom)　, I hope you can tell the joy that it gives all of us here to see your joy, your love for each other.

The road to this moment has been a long and winding one for both of you. That is why the story of Ruth is such a good metaphor of your love. It is the story of two people coming from very different backgrounds, making a commitment to merge the pathways of their lives and continue their journey together.

Like Ruth and Naomi, the past has held both great joy and the pain of great loss for each of you. You will never forget your pasts.

You wouldn't want to. For even in the painful times you experienced, you grew and found strength to live through them with dignity and integrity. They changed you and helped to form you into the person standing here today — the person each of you fell in love with.

So you cannot escape the past, but like Ruth and Naomi, you can move beyond it. It is not the last word. A whole new road called the future is opening up before you. And how we rejoice in your readiness to share the journey into that future with one another!

There may have been times when each of you wondered if you could ever love again. But God has given us an amazing capacity to love and be loved. Our part is to take the risk of trying. Your presence here today tells all of us that that risk is definitely worth taking.

There may be days ahead when you will still wonder if your love is genuine. Go back, then, to Paul's reminder in 1 Corinthians 13 of what God-given love looks like. It's true that not one of us ever lives up fully to Paul's definition. We have a hard time being that selfless. But how wonderful it is in those moments when love does show through as it was meant to be. I pray that you will have many such moments, (Bride) and (Groom) . They will be the building blocks for your love to continue to grow.

This love you have for each other is truly a gift! Cherish the gift. Nurture it with all the time and tender care you can give it. And give thanks always to the Giver, for it is God who made you and will give you all the faith, hope, and love you need to carry out the commitment you are making to one another today.

May God bless your love now and always.

Miracles Of Marriage

Listen to these words from Genesis 2:18-24 (TEV):

Then the Lord God said, "It is not good for the man to live alone. I will make a suitable companion to help him." So he took some soil from the ground and formed all the animals and all the birds. Then he brought them to the man to see what he would name them; and that is how they all got their names. So the man named all the birds and all the animals; but not one of them was a suitable companion to help him.

Then the Lord God made the man fall into a deep sleep and while he was sleeping, he took out one of the man's ribs and closed up the flesh. He formed a woman out of the rib and brought her to him.

Then the man said, "At last, here is one of my own kind — Bone taken from my bone, and flesh from my flesh. 'Woman' is her name because she was taken out of man."

That is why a man leaves his father and mother and is united with his wife, and they become one.

Genesis talks about the beginnings of love between a man and a woman. In the New Testament, Paul writes about how real love can be recognized and nurtured. From 1 Corinthians 13 (NRSV):

Love is patient; love is kind; love is not envious or boastful or arrogant or rude. It does not insist on its own way; it is not irritable or resentful; it does not rejoice in wrongdoing, but rejoices in the truth. It bears all things, believes all things, hopes all things, endures all things.

Love never ends ... When I was a child, I spoke like a child, I thought like a child, I reasoned like a child;

when I became an adult, I put an end to childish ways. For now we see in a mirror, dimly, but then we will see face to face. Now I know only in part; then I will know fully, even as I have been fully known. And now faith, hope, and love abide, these three; and the greatest of these is love.

I don't know if you believe in miracles, __(Bride)__ and __(Groom)__. But if you think of a miracle as a wonder God has brought about, then it is clear that there is a miracle taking place right now. For that is what every loving marriage really is.

It begins with the miracle of recognition. Like Adam in the Garden, sitting there naming all the animals, one by one. Life was all right, mildly entertaining. Then one day he wakes up, looks over and sees this beautiful new creation of God, Eve, and says, "WOW! This is what I've been looking for all along and didn't even know it. This is the one who will be a companion, a partner for me."

Out of all the other women in the world, __(Groom)__, you picked __(Bride)__; out of all the other men in the world, __(Bride)__, you picked __(Groom)__. Somehow you recognized in one another those attributes and attitudes which not only attract you, but which somehow you sense will help each of you to be a better person. I think that is a miracle — the miracle of recognition.

Then there is the miracle of uniting. You are two separate individuals, with your own family traditions, your own habits and ways of doing things, your own individual hopes and dreams. Yet, today, you are ready to bring all of those individual parts of yourselves together into a new entity, a brand new branch off of your two families. As Genesis says, "A man leaves his father and mother, and the two become one."

Of course, you won't leave everything behind. You wouldn't want to. The love of your family is a big part of who you are today. And your unique individuality is what drew you to one another. You don't want to lose either of those, but your focus will be different from now on. Instead of thinking mostly about pleasing your parents or pleasing yourself, your first thought must now be "What will be best for us together?" That any person would even want to do that is what I would call a miracle — the miracle of uniting.

The greatest miracle of all is yet to come. It is the miracle of loving. You may think you already have that, and you have begun. But the kind of loving I hope you will aim for is what Paul talks about in 1 Corinthians. It is more than being a friend to each other. It is more than being lovers. It is love which says, "I am willing to give my life for you." This is the same kind of love Christ has shown for all of us.

Such love does not come to us automatically. It is a gift from God. When you learn to offer that gift of love in your marriage, there will be nothing than can tear you apart, for Christ's love never ends. That is the miracle of loving.

 (Bride) and (Groom) , this day you are experiencing God's miracles. May each day of your life together bring you a fresh awareness of God's love for you and the miracle of your love for each other. God bless you.

Leaving, Uniting, Becoming One

Hear these words from the first book in the Bible, Genesis, chapter 2, verses 18-24 (TEV):

> *Then the Lord God said, "It is not good for the man to live alone. I will make a suitable companion to help him." So [God] took some soil from the ground and formed all the animals and all the birds. Then [God] brought them to the man to see what he would name them; and that is how they all got their names. So the man named all the birds and all the animals; but not one of them was a suitable companion to help him.*
>
> *Then the Lord God made the man fall into a deep sleep, and while he was sleeping, [God] took out one of the man's ribs and closed up the flesh. [God] formed a woman out of the rib and brought her to him. Then the man said, "At last [or loosely translated, "Wow!"], here is one of my own kind — Bone taken from my bone, and flesh from my flesh. 'Woman' is her name because she was taken out of man." That is why a man leaves his father and mother and is united with his wife, and they become one.*

It seemed like God had given the first man everything he needed — a nice place to live, interesting work to do. But that wasn't enough. Something was missing from his life — until God introduced the woman. Then he knew his search was over.

I realize this is a male-dominated story, but we're going to forget for the moment about who was made from whose rib and focus on that last verse, for that is the part that tells us what marriage is all about in God's view. "That is why a man leaves his father and mother and is united with his wife, and they become one."

Leaving, uniting, becoming one — that is what getting married involves, _(Bride)_ and _(Groom)_. Did you realize you were doing all that?

The leaving may seem not to apply. You've both left your parents' homes and established your own independence. But there is another level of leaving that is considerably more challenging. It is when you begin to leave behind your old habits of relating to people. It's the question of who you turn to for emotional support, and even for fun. Are you learning to turn to one another first? Friends and family are great. We need them. They have helped to shape you into the persons you are standing here today. You won't ever stop loving these people and enjoying their company. But how you relate to them will change, for your primary loyalty is to each other now. You are leaving behind the patterns of your past lives to build this new life together.

That is possible because of all the excitement and challenge of uniting as a couple. There are so many ways your lives are being united: not only through your checkbooks, your furniture, and all your other physical belongings, but also through your dreams, your hopes for the future, your individual strengths and weaknesses — your lives.

As with the process of leaving the past behind, that kind of uniting does not happen overnight. Some days you will feel downright selfish, maybe even threatened — as if you might just lose your very self if you have to share one more thing. (I personally draw the line at toothbrushes.) But don't give up, for the reward for all the leaving behind and uniting is discovering the joy of becoming one.

This is not just a sexual oneness, though it includes that. It's not an emotional oneness, though at times you will feel emotionally very much in sync. When a couple becomes one, they begin to see themselves more as a team working together than as two individuals worrying about who is getting the most attention, the most power in decision-making, the most benefit from this marriage. Two become one when each partner thinks of the other person and what he or she needs before thinking of themselves. When each of you is giving 100 percent to the other, watch out! That is when rockets flare and love really blossoms!

So that is what God's idea of marriage is, (Bride) and (Groom) . As you begin your married life together, look to God, the One who made you to love each other, and to Christ, who showed us what unselfish love looks like, and to the Holy Spirit, who gives us the power to love. May our gracious Creator God bless you with a long and happy marriage. Amen.

Growing A Marriage
(for an outdoor setting)

Hear these words about God's idea of love as it has been shown to us in Jesus Christ, and is described in Paul's letter to the Ephesians, chapter 3:14-19 (TEV):

> *For this reason I fall on my knees before the Father, from whom every family in heaven and on earth receives its true name. I ask God from the wealth of his glory to give you power through his Spirit to be strong in your inner selves, and I pray that Christ will make his home in your hearts through faith. I pray that you may have your roots and foundation in love, so that you, together with all God's people, may have the power to understand how broad and long, how high and deep, is Christ's love. Yes, may you come to know his love — although it can never be fully known — and so be completely filled with the very nature of God.*

Your new lawn is coming along nicely. You hoped it would be all filled in by today, but you discovered that growing things just cannot be rushed. It's true of lawns. It's true of trees. It's even true of marriages. It will take time for your marriage to grow strong and beautiful. Lasting love cannot be rushed.

Paul gives us a good image of what love in God's family is like. He was probably likening it to the growth of a tree. But let's change the image just a bit and liken the creation of a healthy marriage to growing a lawn.

First, someone has to get it all started. Someone has to prepare the ground and plant the seeds and help them to grow. Just so, your love for one another didn't just begin when you met one another. It began many years earlier, all the years of your lives up to that point, as you learned what love is — and is not — from those around you. You learned what love is not as you faced the disappointment and pain of marriages that did not last. You learned what love is as you experienced the unconditional love of your parents, your extended family, your friends, and God. These were the ones who helped to plant seeds of love in your hearts. Love grew between the two of you because your hearts had been prepared by love to love.

Now your task is to establish strong roots for your love. Roots are what bring nourishment to keep growing lawns and growing relationships alive and well. A lawn won't grow very well if its roots are too shallow. Your marriage won't grow very strong either if you only concentrate on the surface of living. Take time, _(Bride)_ and _(Groom)_ , to share your dreams and hopes with one another. Don't let your lives get totally consumed by all those daily and weekly little things that always seem to take our attention. Now and then, leave the dishes and the laundry and the lawn mowing, and maybe even all the running around socializing, and spend time talking about things that really matter, like what you want your life together to be like, what you hope people will remember about you when you are gone, how you can add to the good rather than the evil in the world, and how each of you can be a better person, partner, and perhaps some day, parent.

Of course, if a lawn tries to send its roots into dry ground, it won't have much chance of growing, no matter how deep those roots try to go. It needs a constant, reliable source of water for steady growth. Paul talks about God's love being that kind of constant source of nourishment for our lives. On our own, all of us at one time or another have a tendency to run dry as far as love goes. We lose our patience, we get hurt and then we try to get even, we get all caught up in what *we* want, and we forget to listen to and consider the other person. Lawns can take a little bit of dryness, and so can marriages. But too much dryness and things can begin to look stressed. _(Bride)_ and _(Groom)_ , that is not what God desires for your marriage. Sink your roots deep into the love of God, for God's love never runs dry. It has the power to nourish your lives with more love than you ever thought possible.

Isn't it great how a lawn looks and feels when it is well tended? It is a refreshing oasis in our concrete world. That is what I pray your marriage will be like. You will be amazed how others will draw near to be refreshed in the presence of your love. Genuine love has a way of gently refreshing all who come near. May your lives be filled with that kind of healthy, growing love always. God be with you.

Beginning A New Climb
(for a marriage after divorce)

Hear these words of Scripture as they are found in Paul's letter to the Ephesians, chapter 3:14-19 (TEV):

> *For this reason I fall on my knees before the Father, from whom every family in heaven and on earth receives its true name. I ask God from the wealth of his glory to give you power through his Spirit to be strong in your inner selves, and I pray that Christ will make his home in your hearts through faith. I pray that you may have your roots and foundation in love, so that you, together with all God's people, may have the power to understand how broad and long, how high and deep, is Christ's love. Yes, may you come to know his love — although it can never be fully known — and so be completely filled with the very nature of God.*

 (Bride) and (Groom) , we didn't make it to a mountaintop for your wedding, but think of this as the first step from base camp to climb another mountain called "marriage."

You've already both come a long way to this point. You know from experience the dangers and difficulties of making such a climb. You have both suffered the pain of a first attempt that did not work.

But God's grace abounds. God's Spirit replenishes and renews broken hearts, and teaches them how to love again. So here you are, ready to begin a whole new challenge together as partners in a journey.

What will you need for this climb to be successful? Paul provides some clues in Ephesians.

First, you each need to remain strong in your inner selves. Through all the ups and downs of your individual lives, each of you has learned to be resourceful, competent, and able to handle life fairly well. God's Spirit has been at work in you, helping you not only to survive but to flourish as individuals.

Are you now going to throw all that away and lose yourself in another? No, that's not what lasting love is all about. Marriage is bringing those strengths (and weaknesses) in your inner selves and offering them to one another for the good of your life together. You will be changed by that. The ironic part is, the more you offer of yourself, the more you will discover who you really are. What joy there is in being loved and accepted for ourselves!

A second tip from Ephesians: let Christ's love be your safety line. There will be times when you stumble in the climb toward a lasting marriage. You will get tired, distracted, discouraged. At those times, check that safety line — are you staying connected to God? For God's love is ultimately what will hold you up and hold the two of you together, especially when you grow weary.

Finally, don't forget to stop now and then and take a look at the view. How sad to think of a marriage as a climb in which you plod along with only grit and determination. It is the moments of fun and inspiration that often make the difference in being able to take the next step forward. Stop and notice how far you have come as a couple. Celebrate that with each other, in big and little ways. Look around and join with all God's people in thanking God for the mystery and wonder of Christ's love, which is so broad and long, so high and deep.

It's a big mountain that stands before you, __(Bride)__ and __(Groom)__ — this mountain called marriage. But joined together with God, may the climb be more thrilling than you ever imagined. God be with you.

Rooted In Love

(for a blended family)

Hear these words about God's idea of love as it has been shown to us in Jesus Christ, and is described in Paul's letter to the Ephesians, chapter 3:14-19 (TEV):

> *For this reason I fall on my knees before the Father, from whom every family in heaven and on earth receives its true name. I ask God from the wealth of his glory to give you power through his Spirit to be strong in your inner selves, and I pray that Christ will make his home in your hearts through faith. I pray that you may have your roots and foundation in love, so that you, together with all God's people, may have the power to understand how broad and long, how high and deep, is Christ's love. Yes, may you come to know his love — although it can never be fully known — and so be completely filled with the very nature of God.*

   (Bride) and (Groom) , we celebrate the new family that is being officially formed here today. We celebrate the love that grew between the two of you, until finally you decided: this is it; we don't want to live separate lives; we want to become one family. We're glad for your willingness to make this permanent commitment to one another. What a great gift of love that is for you to give to one another, and also to (*Children's names*). For as they see you two caring about and for each other, as they see you showing love in the way you treat each other with respect and consideration, and as you include them in that love and caring, they will be strengthened, along with you, by the love you are sharing.

Paul gives us a good picture of what love in God's family is like. It's a lot like a tree. Now a tree is only as strong as its roots. For the roots are what bring food and water to the rest of it to keep everything alive and working. A tree can't grow very strong if its roots are too shallow. Your marriage won't grow very strong either if you only concentrate on the surface of living. Take time, _(Bride)_ and _(Groom)_ , to share your dreams and hopes with one another. Don't let your lives get totally consumed by all those daily and weekly little things that always seem to take our attention. Now and then, leave the dishes, the laundry, the lawn mowing, and the checkbook balancing, and spend time talking about things that really matter: like what you want your family to be like, what you hope people will remember about you when you're gone, how you can add to the good rather than the evil in the world, and how you can be a better person, partner, and parent.

Of course, if a tree tries to sink its roots into dry ground, it won't have much chance of growing, no matter how deep those roots try to go. It needs a constant, reliable source of water for steady growth. Paul talks about God's love being that kind of constant source of nourishment for our spirits. On our own, all of us at one time or another run out of the ability to love. Our hearts seem to run dry. We lose our patience; we get hurt and then we try to get even; we get all caught up in what *we* want, and forget to listen to and consider the other person. Over time that's what makes a lot of marriages dry up and become lifeless. God wants so much more for you. I pray that you will sink your family's roots into God's great love. For God's love never runs dry. God has the power to fill your lives with more love than you ever thought possible.

(Bride) and _(Groom)_ , sink your roots deep into the love of God and let your life together grow into something strong and beautiful. Like a healthy tree whose branches provide shade and fruit for all who come near, family and friends will enjoy being near you, for the love you share will refresh their lives. Then you will know what Paul was talking about: how broad and long, how high and deep is Christ's love. May your lives be filled with that kind of love always. God be with you.

Love — Gift Of God

(for a couple with a baby)

Listen to these words of Scripture from the First Letter of John, chapter 4, verses 7-12 (TEV):

> *Dear friends, let us love one another, because love comes from God. Whoever loves is a child of God and knows God. Whoever does not love does not know God, for God is love. And God showed his love for us by sending his only Son into the world, so that we might have life through him. This is what love is: it is not that we have loved God, but that he loved us and sent his Son to be the means by which our sins are forgiven.*
>
> *Dear friends, if this is how God loved us, then we should love one another. No one has ever seen God, but it we love one another, God lives in union with us, and his love is made perfect in us.*

  (Bride) and (Groom) , remember all those years that you lived in the same neighborhood, but never dreamed you would be standing here like this, ready to promise yourselves to one another in marriage? Back then you were just the boy, the girl, who lived down the block. It's truly amazing how love can begin and grow from such almost unnoticed beginnings.

We all rejoice that you are here! Finally, your love has matured to the point where you want to share it with the world. You are ready to make a permanent commitment to each other and seal it with special vows of faithfulness and caring, witnessed by all these family and friends.

You have put a great deal of time, thought, and effort into preparing for this day. Why? Could it be because you are beginning to realize how important and precious this gift of love is which you are giving to each other?

It is a gift that you will need to keep giving to each other again and again. Just saying how much you love one another as you stand here today won't be enough. In fact, the words, "I love you," will never be enough alone. The author of 1 John states a great truth when he writes in chapter 3, "My children, our love should not be just words and talk; it must be true love, which shows itself in action."

When you stop what you are doing and take time to listen carefully to your partner, that is an act of true love. When you take your turn entertaining a cranky, teething baby, that is an act of true love. When you give an unexpected hug, make a special meal, leave a little love note — those are the kind of small actions which often speak louder than words of your love for each other. They show how much you value the gift of love you have been given.

At this moment, you may feel like this love is a gift only the two of you share. Not so! True love cannot be contained — it has a way of overflowing and touching the lives of all those around you. But right now I want you to think about one very special person your love is affecting. As you nurture your love for one another, you are giving your child a tremendous gift also. For he/she will learn his/her first lessons about love as he/she watches your relationship. Your honesty, openness, and affection toward each other — or the lack of them — will be a powerful example for him/her. As you shower him/her with love, don't forget to keep showering love on each other too. It will add to his/her sense of security, and it will be an important way of passing on God's gift of love to him/her.

On those days when you feel overwhelmed by all of this, when you are just not sure you have another loving action or word in you, remember that love is not something we manufacture ourselves. As 1 John 4 says, love is from God. Our love is renewed when we turn to God, the Source and Power behind all love.

Your love is a gift from God, __(Bride)__ and __(Groom)__. Rejoice in it, nurture it, share it with your little one, and remember always to thank the Giver. May the love of God remain with you always. Amen.

Garments Of Marriage
(for a formal wedding)

Hear these words as they are found in Paul's letter to the Colossians, Chapter 3:12-14 (TEV):

> *You are the people of God; he loved you and chose you for [God's] own. So then, you must clothe yourselves with compassion, kindness, humility, gentleness, and patience. Be tolerant with one another and forgive one another whenever any one of you has a complaint against someone else. You must forgive one another just as the Lord has forgiven you. And to all these qualities add love, which binds all things together in perfect unity.*

Here you are, _(Bride)_ and _(Groom)_, all dressed up in your very best. What you are wearing today makes a statement about the importance of what is happening. It says you desire to bring the very best that you have and the best that you are to this wedding service, because that's what you want to bring to your married life together. The only thing is, these clothes are not exactly what you're going to be wearing day in and day out. Have you seen any brides and grooms changing the oil in their car, mowing the lawn or doing the laundry in the kind of clothes you're wearing today? We all know that when it comes to daily living, we have to put on clothes that stand up to the demands of ordinary life.

The same is true of the actions and attitudes which you bring to your marriage. On this, your wedding day, you stand before each other with all the love and affection, the respect and caring that is within you for one another. It's a beautiful thing to see. It shines on your faces. It shows in your eyes. That's why people love to watch brides and grooms on their wedding day.

But you know each other well enough to realize that life is not one continuous wedding day. What are the actions and attitudes that will wear well for the two of you when you have to get back to the hard work of daily living? After the wedding clothes are put away, with what garments will you clothe your heart?

The Apostle Paul seemed to have a good handle on human nature. Though he wrote his letter to a church family, his words are worth holding onto for the new relationship you two are creating through your marriage. First Paul says to bring these attitudes to your relationship: *compassion*, the ability to put yourself in the other person's shoes and feel what your partner is feeling; *kindness*, that willingness to do those little things that show your partner that you really value him or her, whether it's that extra hug on your way by, or folding the laundry so the other one doesn't have to; *humility*, not seeing yourself as even the tiniest little bit better than your spouse, but realizing even you yourself have areas of your life that need some help; *gentleness*, the awareness that no matter how tough we all act on the outside, our spirits are easily wounded and need the tenderest, loving care; and *patience*, the gracious attitude of hoping for the very best from one another, but not giving up when change comes slowly.

Paul mentions all these attitudes, but only one action. That one action is to forgive. Until that day when one of you becomes perfect — don't hold your breath — you will need to forgive one another. Forgiveness doesn't mean letting people get away with anything they want to do. Forgiveness is letting people know that we love them too much to remind them forever of the mistakes they've made. There is no freedom like the freedom forgiveness brings.

Now Paul knew that all these things require a kind of self-forgetting that we are not inclined to practice very often. So, he says, we need to wrap all these attitudes and action in love. Your love for each other, _(Bride)_ and _(Groom)_, will give you the energy and desire to show compassion, kindness, humility, gentleness, patience, and forgiveness to one another.

But your love alone won't make this happen. Human love has a way of fading in and out, unless it finds its Source. And the Source of all love is God. Let God be your unseen Partner, helping you to create a marriage relationship of lasting, loving beauty that will wear well forever. This day, let your wedding gift to one another be these garments of the heart, wrapped in love, and worn with thankfulness to God. May God bless you both.